WETLANDS
PLANTS AND ANIMALS
Coloring Book

Annika Bernhard

DOVER PUBLICATIONS, INC.
New York

Bibliographical Note

Wetlands Plants and Animals Coloring Book is a new work, first published by Dover Publications, Inc., in 1994.

DOVER *Pictorial Archive* SERIES

International Standard Book Number: 0-486-27749-6

Manufactured in the United States of America
Dover Publications, Inc., 31 East 2nd Street, Mineola, N.Y. 11501

PUBLISHER'S NOTE

ONCE MARSHES, SWAMPS AND BOGS—collectively called *wetlands*—were regarded as nuisances, fit only to be drained for farming.

Only now, when about half of all U.S. wetlands have been destroyed, have we come to realize that usually wetlands are most valuable—economically as well as environmentally—when left alone.

The waterlogged soil of wetlands, particularly of marshes, is rich in nutrients and forms the breeding and feeding grounds for many species of birds, mammals, amphibians, reptiles, fishes and insects. Not their least value is their use as buffers against flooding and storm damage. They also aid in maintaining the level of groundwater in neighboring territory. Thus swamps and marshes are extremely valuable to the most developed of human settlements as well as to the sustenance of lower forms of life.

This coloring book depicts several dozen of the most common species of plants and animals found in saltmarshes of the Northeast Coast, among the most extensive and interesting wetlands in the world. Similar marshlands may be found in other parts of the U.S. and elsewhere; they are simply most highly concentrated in the Northeast.

Subject to periodic flooding by saltwater, the effects of which few land plants can survive, the border of land and water that forms the distinctive part of a saltmarsh is a hostile environment. Those creatures that have adapted are rewarded by the abundance of nutrients and relative absence of competitors. The comparatively small but distinctive group of water and land plants, birds, mammals, amphibians, reptiles, fishes, crustaceans, mollusks, insects and yet other creatures—some well known, like muskrats and herons, others, like certain inconspicuous worms and snails, poorly known except to specialists—that regularly inhabit saltmarshes form a fascinating lot that have learned to coexist for thousands of years. Many other fish, mammals and other animals regularly visit saltmarshes.

Highly recommended supplementary reading (and the source of some of the information in the captions to the drawings and this note) is the classic study by John and Mildred Teal, *Life and Death of the Salt Marsh* (New York: Ballantine Books, 1971).

A number of the drawings are shown in color on the covers, and alphabetical lists of common and of Latin names appear at the back of the book.

1. **Saltmeadow Cordgrass** (*Spartina patens*). Closely related to Saltmarsh Cordgrass (see pages 6, 20, 21 and 22), this grass is also resistant to the harsh, withering effects of immersion in saltwater, but less so. Able to survive only occasional inundation, it grows on higher ground. It was once harvested by farmers for hay.

2. **American Eel** (*Anguilla rostrata*). This is the only
North American freshwater eel. It enters saltwater—
including marshes—at breeding time.

3. **Snowy Egret** (*Egretta thula*). Thanks to pioneering conservation efforts, this beautiful bird, once nearly hunted to extinction for its plumage, has made a glorious comeback. It is now quite common in saltmarshes.

4. **Raccoon** (*Procyon lotor*). The omnivorous Raccoon needs no introduction. It relishes the various kinds of food it can scrounge in saltmarshes as much as any it finds in woodlands or city garbage cans. **Common European Periwinkle** (*Littorina littorea*). Despite its name, this common snail is also found along the coast of northeastern North America. **Mosquitofish** (*Gambusia affinis*). This small live-bearing fish (it does not lay eggs) has been widely introduced in fresh and brackish water to help control mosquitoes (it eats the larvae).

5. **Purple Marsh Crab** (*Sesarma reticulatum*). This is a member of a group of crabs that build mud huts in marshlands from which they venture out in search of food.

Brown-banded Wentletrap (*Epitonium rupicola*). This snail (to the left of the crab) also lives near, rather than directly in, saltmarshes. It associates with sea anemones.

6. **Clapper Rail** (*Rallus longirostris*). Common, though rarely seen because (like most of the rails) it is so secretive, the Clapper Rail is perfectly at home in the tall grasses of saltmarshes, where it finds its food as well as cover from potential predators. **Saltmarsh Cordgrass** (*Spartina alterniflora*). If there is one plant that is essential to saltmarshes, this is it. For more information, see pages 20, 21 and 22.

7. **Rockweed** (*Fucus vesiculosus*). A type of brown seaweed found in tidal areas. **Clam Worm** (*Nereis limbata*). One of a group of creatures called the segmented worms, the Clam Worm lives near sandy shores and eats any small creatures it can capture with its sharp pincers. In turn it is eaten by fish.

8. **Green Striped Grasshopper** (*Hesperotettix viridis*). A vegetarian that eats grass, and related to the many other grasshoppers of fields and meadows, this one is often found in saltmarshes.

9. **Least Tern** (*Sterna antillarum*). This smallest North American tern dives for small fish in marshy waters. **Perennial Saltmarsh Aster** (*Aster tenuifolius*). Closely related to the asters so popular in horticulture, this plant (foreground) is found only in saltmarshes in the Northeast.

10. **Mosquito** (*family Culicidae*). There is hardly a spot of land on earth where at least one of the world's 2,500 species of mosquitoes doesn't live to torment and transmit diseases to humans and other animals. They are particularly associated with marshes because they readily breed in tidal pools, as in any standing water. Despite their annoying and dangerous characteristics, however, mosquitoes do furnish a source of food for numerous fish, birds and other insects (such as dragonflies). Eggs (left) and larvae are shown here in the water.

11. **Great Blue Heron** (*Ardea herodias*). This large, stately wading bird finds itself at home in wetlands of all kinds throughout nearly all of North America. It feeds on fish, frogs and other small creatures.

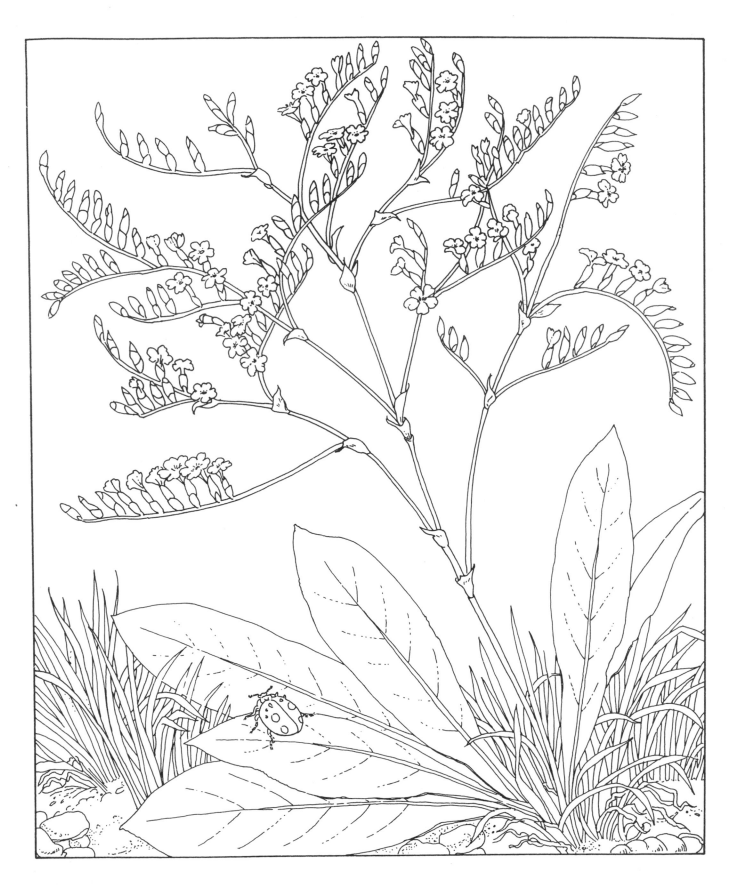

12. **Sea Lavender** (*Limonium carolinianum*). In late summer and fall, clusters of these plants with lavender-colored flowers are prominent in coastal marshes. **Ladybug** (or Ladybird Beetle) (family Coccinellidae). Most of these beetles (actually a family of thousands of species) eat aphids and other small insects destructive to plants; this fact coupled with their attractive coloration has made the Ladybug a favorite insect of many people.

13. **Hermit Crab** (family Paguridae). Hermit crabs are any of a number of related species of crabs that adopt snail shells as their own. When they outgrow a shell, they simply find a slightly larger one and move in! **Widgeongrass** (*Ruppia maritima*). Related to the pondweeds, this underwater plant is an important source of food for migrating waterfowl. Also of special note is its ability to survive in a highly alkaline environment.

14. **Atlantic Horseshoe Crab** (*Limulus polyphemus*). Not really crabs, these ancient creatures have inhabited the sea in essentially the same form since the days of the dinosaurs and are closely related to now-extinct creatures even older. In the spring, Atlantic Horseshoe Crabs crawl up by the thousands on the shores of beaches and marshes on the Atlantic and Gulf Coasts to lay eggs by the billions. Most of these eggs never hatch—they are eaten by thousands of gulls and shorebirds specially arrived for the feast. **Beach Grass** (*Ammophila breviligulata*). Growing just out of reach of the devastating effects of the tides, Beach Grass (top) is important for preventing the erosion of land on higher ground surrounding saltmarshes.

15. **Black Skimmer** (*Rynchops niger*). This is the North American representative of the only group of birds in the world that has a bill with a lower mandible longer than the upper, a feature that enables the Black Skimmer to "skim" food from the surface as it flies close to the water. **Sea-Myrtle** (*Baccharis halimifolia*). This white-flowered shrub, a northerly representative of a mostly tropical family, is found on the borders of coastal marshes.

16. **Osprey** (*Pandion haliaetus*). Not long ago, the Osprey was in serious trouble as a result of DDT poisoning; now this spectacular fish-hunting hawk is making a strong comeback. Found in suitable habitat throughout much of the world, the Osprey eats mostly fish, which it catches by dramatically plunging into the water. **Common Barnacle** (*Balanus balanus*). This well-known sea dweller, though related to shrimps and crabs, at an early stage of its life permanently attaches itself to such solid objects as timber, ships and rocks, and feeds by filtering organic matter from the surrounding water.

17. **Black-bellied Plover** (*Pluvialis squatarola*). Though not as amazing a long-distance flier as its cousin the Golden Plover, the Black-bellied Plover still covers considerable ground in its migration from the Arctic to the United States, where it winters. It feeds on the small creatures found on the shores of marshes and elsewhere near water. **Seaside Goldenrod** (*Solidago sempervirens*). This beautiful yellow-flowered plant is most conspicuous in the fall.

18. **Sea Lettuce** (*Ulva lactuca*). This common form of seaweed often washes ashore in saltmarshes, conspicuous because of its bright green color. **Atlantic Ribbed Mussel** (*Modiolus demissus*). This is the most common form of shellfish in North America, although—or more probably *because*—it is considered inedible by humans. Nevertheless, it is a delicacy to marsh residents as different as raccoons and gulls.

19. **Ruddy Turnstone** (*Arenaria interpres*). This bright orange-black-and-white-patterned shorebird prefers to find its food in rocky areas. It is one of the major consumers of Horseshoe Crab eggs in season. **Great Bulrush** (*Scirpus validus*). This tall, widespread marsh plant is neither a rush nor a grass but is in the sedge family.

20–21. Panoramic View of a Saltmarsh. If there is one form of life in this picture more essential to the character and survival of the saltmarsh than any other, it is a grass, **Saltmarsh Cordgrass** (*Spartina alterniflora;* see also pages 6 and 22). Because it has evolved a resistance to persistent and repeated immersion in saltwater, this grass thrives where no other plant can. It helps keep the places where it grows resistant to erosion, provides shelter for

numerous visitors from the air, land and water, and when it decays fills the marsh with nutrients that form the foundation of a large and important food chain. In addition to Saltmarsh Cordgrass, this drawing also shows many of the other creatures that call the saltmarsh home. Most are also shown and described in the other drawings in this book. How many can you identify?

22. **Saltmarsh Cordgrass** (*Spartina alterniflora*). This essential saltmarsh plant (see also pages 6, 20 and 21) is able to survive repeated immersion in saltwater by having evolved a complex biochemical system whereby it retains salt in some portions of its structure while excreting excess salt from others. "Spartina," as it is often called from its Latin name, works very hard to survive the effects of the tides, but in this way is able to survive in a hostile environment that very few other land plants can endure. **Fiery Skipper** (*Hylephilia phyleus*). One of hundreds of small butterflies called Skippers, this tiny orange-and-brown butterfly (top) loves grasses. **Black Horsefly** (*Tabanus atratus*). This large biting fly is a nuisance to many animals, not merely horses.

23. **Laughing Gull** (*Larus atricilla*). This noisy, medium-size gull is conspicuous at breeding time because of its black head and laughlike call. Like the Ruddy Turnstone, it is a major consumer of Horseshoe Crab eggs in season; out of season, like most gulls, it happily consumes all kinds of food, though it is not so much a scavenger as some of its cousins. **Marsh Mallow** (*Hibiscus moscheutos*). Not only is this Hibiscus (left) lovely for its white flowers, this is the plant a gummy extract of which served as the original marshmallow confection many decades ago.

24. **Blue Crab** (*Callinectes sapidus*). These attractively colored swimming crabs (lower left) of the Atlantic and Gulf coasts often find their way into saltmarshes—to their detriment, for they are among the most sought-after shell-fish for the kitchen. The young crabs whose shells have not hardened are harvested and sold as "soft-shell" crabs. **Striped Mullet** (*Mugil cephalus*). This common and im-portant food fish (background) travels in large schools. Its own food consists heavily of plant matter abundantly found in saltmarshes. **Blood Worm** (*Glycera dibranchiata*). An annelid (segmented) worm related to the Clam Worm, the Blood Worm (lower right) is popularly used as bait in fishing.

25. **Common Blue Mussel** (*Mytilus edulis*). As its name suggests, this smooth-shelled mussel is very common, found attached to rocks and pilings all along the East Coast. **Eelgrass** (*Zostera marina*). Like its close relative Widgeongrass, Eelgrass is an underwater plant much favored by waterfowl.

26. **Green-backed Heron** (*Butorides striatus*). This small wading bird is a common resident of marshes, where it eats fish, frogs, worms, and other creatures. **Bay Anchovy** (*Anchoa mitchilli*). Member of a commercially valuable family, the Bay Anchovy (bottom) is the North American species of this small schooling fish that is most commonly found in saltmarshes. **Eastern Mud Nassa** (*Ilynassa obsoleta*). This common snail (lower right) buries itself in the mud and eats whatever it can filter out of the water. It will emerge from its mud home, however, to scavenge on dead fish.

27. Widow Skimmer (Dragonfly) (*Libellula luctosa*). One of many species of dragonflies, this nimble flier, like all of its family, is a predatory insect. From our point of view, its predations are totally unobjectionable, since dragonflies love to eat mosquitoes!

28. **American Lobster** (*Homarus americanus*). This well-loved crustacean, so familiar from the dinner table, is actually colored a dark green in nature. It assumes the bright red color by which it is popularly known only after having been boiled!

29. **Short-billed Dowitcher** (*Limnodromus griseus*). This sandpiper is "short-billed" only by comparison with its more westerly long-billed cousin. It digs in the mud with a distinctive up-and-down motion to obtain the small marine creatures on which it subsists. **Swamp Rose Mallow** (*Hibiscus palustris*). This Hibiscus with showy pink flowers (right) is closely related to the Marsh Mallow (see page 23); some botanists consider them to be varieties of the same species.

30. **Seahorse** (family Syngnathidae). Seahorses are of course in no way related to horses—these odd members of the pipefish family just resemble them. Besides their appearance, another characteristic of these fish makes them unusual: the male hatches the female's eggs in a special pouch and holds the young there until they are ready to fend for themselves (Seahorses might for this reason well be called "Sea Kangaroos"!).

31. **Red-winged Blackbird** (*Agelaius phoeniceus*). This raucous bird is a familiar inhabitant of salt- and freshwater wetlands throughout North America. Only the male displays the color pattern of its name; female Red-winged Blackbirds are neither red-winged nor black, looking rather like large brown sparrows! **Soft Rush** (*Juncus effusus*). This grasslike plant is actually a close relative of the lilies.

32. **Mayfly** (nymph and adult) (order Ephemerida). The Mayfly (top) is among the few living creatures that do not eat anything as adults—they live just long enough to mate and produce new Mayflies, never longer than a day or two! The nymphs, or larval-stage insects, live in fresh or brackish water for up to two years (see bottom of drawing). They are a favorite food of fish. **Green Crab** (*Carcinides maenas*). This is an attractive-looking swimming crustacean (left) that hides under rocks. **Atlantic Spadefish** (*Chaetodipterus faber*). This schooling fish (right) feeds mostly on plants and small invertebrates.

33. **Mallard** (*Anas platyrhynchos*). Without doubt the best-known duck in the world, the Mallard (bottom) has been widely introduced where it does not occur naturally. **American Black Duck** (*Anas rubripes*). So closely related to the Mallard that the two species hybridize readily, this duck (upper left) has a much more restricted range. **Sea Oats** (*Uniola paniculata*). Few grasses present a more graceful appearance waving in the wind than Sea Oats, found on coastal dunes. Its range is more southerly than that of most of the other plants in these drawings.

34. **Northern Harrier** (*Circus cyaneus*). Also called the Marsh Hawk, this graceful bird of prey will soar over marshes for hours at a time in search of the various small creatures that are its food.

35. **Marsh Wren** (*Cistothorus palustris*). As its name implies, this spunky little bird is at home in both fresh- and saltwater marshes, building its nests in dense clusters of reeds.

36. Seaside Sparrow (*Ammodramus maritimus*). A sparrow thoroughly adapted to life on the shore, this bird eats small creatures typically found in a saltmarsh environment.

Large Marsh Pink (*Sabatia dodecandra*). One of the loveliest marsh residents, this plant produces showy pink flowers through the summer months.

37. **Greater Yellowlegs** (*Tringa melanoleuca*). This long-legged shorebird is one of the most common and familiar of the sandpipers. **Purple Gerardia** (*Agalinis purpurea*). The beautiful purple flowers of this plant (lower left) generally last only through the morning. Gerardias are partly parasitic, tapping where they can the nutrients from the roots of neighboring plants.

38. **Muskrat** (*Ondatra zibethicus*). Muskrats build their own houses of grasses and other plants found near water. They readily feed on any number of plants and small animals found in saltmarshes.

39. **Summer Flounder** (*Paralichthys dentatus*). This flatfish, popularly known to fishermen as the fluke, will breed in or near saltmarshes, where the fry find plenty of food to nourish them until they can swim farther out to sea. **Sand Shrimp** (*Crago vulgaris*). This common shrimp (lower left) lives in large numbers on the muddy bottoms of saltmarshes.

Particularly favored by flounder, the Sand Shrimp is an important link in the saltmarsh food chain. **Scud** (*Gammarus locusta*). These often inconspicuous creatures (upper right), related to Beach Fleas, find their food under stones and seaweed.

40. **Monarch** (*Danaus plexippus*). Probably the best-known butterfly in North America, the Monarch is one of the few migrating insects (unlike birds, however, no individual butterfly lives long enough to make a complete round trip!). Most East Coast Monarchs winter in Mexico. **Reed Grass** (*Phragmites communis*). This tall grass (left), introduced from the Old World, has become very common in saltmarshes. Far less valuable than the Spartina grasses, it nevertheless provides shelter for numerous small creatures. **Slender Glasswort** (*Salicornia europaea*). The Glassworts (right) are particularly well adapted to saltmarshes as their seed will germinate in very salty water, a rarity in the vegetable world.

41. **Least Sandpiper** (*Calidris minutilla*). As its name suggests, this is the smallest North American sandpiper. It will feed on any number of small creatures found in the mud. **Silverweed** (*Potentilla anserina*). This hardy member of the Cinquefoil family is frequently found in saltmarshes. It has bright yellow flowers (bottom).

42. Semipalmated Plover (*Charadrius semipalmatus*). This common shorebird migrates hundreds, even thousands of miles a year to and from its Arctic and sub-Arctic breeding grounds. It frequently stops to feed in coastal marshes. **Fiddler Crab** (*Uca minax*). No crab is more dis- tinctive than the Fiddler (bottom), the male of which sports a huge claw that functions specially in courtship rituals. **Sea Milkwort** (*Glaux maritima*). This is another of the few plants that thrive in a salty environment. It has small but attractive pink flowers (bottom left).

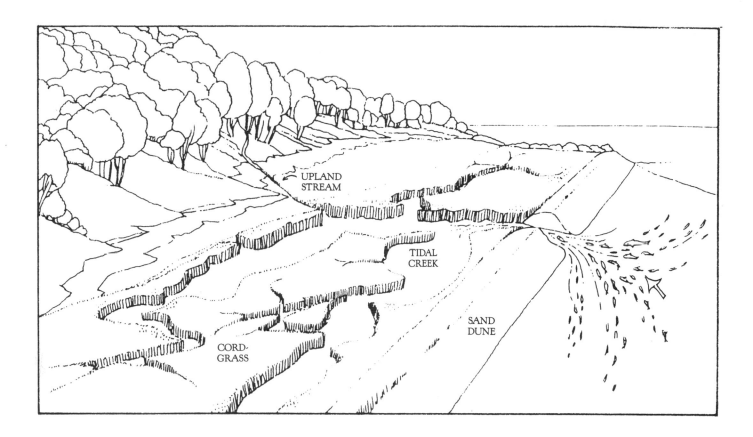

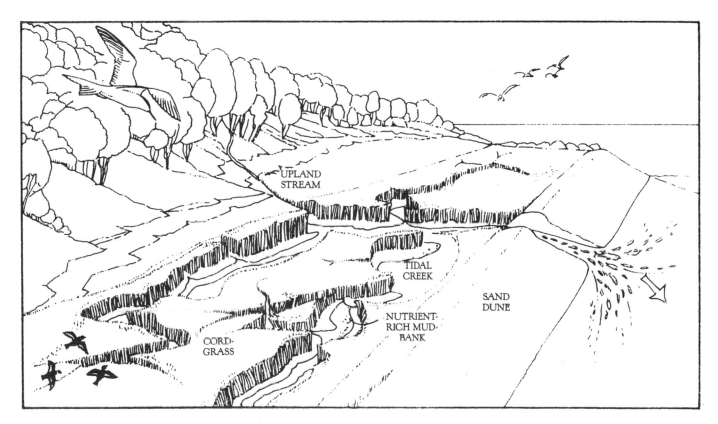

43. TOP: Coastal saltmarsh as the tide flows in.
BOTTOM: Coastal saltmarsh as the tide flows out.

ALPHABETICAL LIST OF COMMON NAMES

ALPHABETICAL LIST OF SCIENTIFIC NAMES